Summary of

The Innovator's Dilemma

When New Technologies Cause
Great Firms to Fail

by Clayton M. Christensen

Instaread

Please Note

This is a summary with analysis.

Table of Contents

Overview

The Innovator's Dilemma contemplates the difficulties of maintaining a firm's position when faced with innovative technologies. It was first published in 1997 and remains an influential text for its descriptions of the reasons that some of the most successful firms in a given business often rapidly lose market share to new challengers.

Large companies that spend millions on research and development often fail to effectively confront challenges posed by innovation. Traditional business practices such as conducting strategic planning and paying close attention to customer needs are insufficient for negotiating disruptive innovations in the market. This is the innovator's dilemma. Business managers must be prepared to confront this paradox. Rather than specific suggestions, they require a theoretical framework to manage the impact of disruptive innovation on established firms.

The history of the disk drive industry from the 1970s into the mid-1990s suggests that business innovations can come in two forms: innovations that help established firms maintain their advantages, and disruptive innovations that can rapidly transform an industry. Disruptive innovation is likely to come in the guise of a low-cost product that initially appeals only to a few consumers. The disruptive innovation gains customers in its market by providing a cheaper and more convenient alternative. Disruptive innovation is a relentless process, so established firms must be prepared to confront disruption when it occurs in their markets.

Important People

Clayton M. Christensen is a former business consultant and is professor of business administration at the Harvard Business School.

Key Takeaways

1. Improvements to a new technology are easy at first but become more difficult to achieve over time.

2. Technological innovations can be divided into two types: sustaining innovations and disruptive innovations.

3. Disruptive innovations are often able to earn a place in the market by focusing on price point.

4. Listening to customers and responding to their wishes can actually be counterproductive. Disruptive innovations create their own markets.

5. While market research is a key part of product development in large firms, it is impossible to do market research with customers and clients of new technologies.

6. Market dynamics can favor new entrants into a business's sector at the expense of well-established firms.

7. Large companies are bureaucratic. Innovation within them is often difficult as a result.

8. Defectors who leave successful companies to start rival firms can be a serious challenge to the position of established firms in the market.

Thank you for purchasing this Instaread book

**Download the Instaread mobile app to get
unlimited text & audio summaries
of bestselling books.**

Visit Instaread.co
to learn more.

Analysis

Key Takeaway 1

Improvements to a new technology are easy at first but become more difficult to achieve over time.

Analysis

When a new technology is developed, the initial improvements to that technology come readily. Over time, new developments become more difficult for research efforts to achieve. An initial breakthrough, whether by luck or by research, leads to a product's commercial viability. Customer feedback provides a guide, and small changes can be made in the design at little cost. This can lead to a steady rate of improvement for some technologies with new versions being released on a regular schedule. Thereafter, research leads to diminishing marginal returns. Improvements can be made, but they cost more time and effort to achieve. The slowing pace of innovation can inspire rival products.

The history of Velcro offers an example. Velcro was first patented in 1955. The Velcro company initially used cotton for its product before quickly discovering that nylon cloth improved the product's performance. The next innovation in the product's history was the use of colored Velcro in the late 1950s. Since these two early product innovations, new uses and developments have been rare, though the brief appeal of Velcro shoes in the 1980s and the Velcro Wall in the 1990s suggests innovations and market opportunities for the product do continue to occur. Instead, the Velcro company has had to increasingly compete with similar lower-cost products from rival firms. [1]

Key Takeaway 2

Technological innovations can be divided into two types: sustaining innovations and disruptive innovations.

Analysis

Although all innovations cause some disruption, not all innovations are categorically disruptive. Some technological innovations sustain the role of incumbents in the market by helping established firms maintain their mainstream customers. Disruptive innovations weaken the hold of established firms; they are more likely to focus on developing fringe features that appeal to only a few customers.

A new innovation can be sustaining to one industry but disruptive to others. Electric cars are a potentially disruptive innovation for traditional automobile manufacturers and gas stations. They are also a sustaining innovation for the highway construction industry or the automobile insurance industry. When determining whether an innovation is sustaining or disruptive, it is better to judge its impact, rather than its design. No matter how revolutionary in design, a new product is not a disruptive innovation unless it potentially threatens the role of established players in a market.

Key Takeaway 3

Disruptive innovations are often able to earn a place in the market by focusing on price point.

Analysis

From the 1970s into the 1990s, the technical specifications of disk drives changed as the price per megabyte paid by consumers was driven lower in each new generation of technology. Throughout its history, innovation in the disk-drive industry largely consisted of repackaging existing technologies in new ways that led to steady reductions in prices per megabyte. The first external hard disk, completed in 1956, was bigger than a refrigerator. Despite its size, this device could only store five megabytes' worth of data. [2] By 1980, five megabytes of data could be stored on a single 5.25-inch disk. [3] In the 1980s 3.5-inch super disks were released capable of storing 10 megabytes of data. [4] Thus, innovation continued to drive down the price per megabyte of storage and resulted in physically smaller drives.

However, development of the 1.8-inch disk drive was at first ignored by major disk-drive producers, which opened opportunities for new manufacturers and technologies to enter the market. Many disk drives and external storage drives became obsolete as new technologies including flash drives and CD-ROM technology entered the market. During this era, computer technology changed quickly. It was not uncommon in the mid-1990s for personal computers on the American market to include both a 3.5-inch disk drive and a CD-ROM rather than the smaller disk drive. While 3.5 disks were re-writable in a way CD-ROMS were not, CDs were cheaper to produce and could store far more data. The growth of CD-ROM market soon made most other disk drives obsolete. [5]

New entrants cannot compete with established companies in terms of product quality and instead often focus on specific features to gain market share. Even if established technologies retain core quality advantage, they can lose customers to disruptive products when coupled with a competitive price. An example is the video cassette recording wars of the 1980s, in which the Betamax format was surpassed by the VHS format. The Betamax format, which predated the development of VHS, had higher picture quality than VHS format tapes. [6] But VHS tapes were slightly cheaper than Betamax tapes. Additionally, VHS tapes could hold longer films than the early generations of Betamax tapes, and this became a decisive factor in consumer preferences. The ability to fit an entire feature-length movie on a single tape became more important to consumers than other factors, such as picture quality.

Key Takeaway 4

Listening to customers and responding to their wishes can actually be counterproductive. Disruptive innovations create their own markets.

Analysis

In traditional business management, analyzing customer feedback is considered important to ensure a company stays relevant to its customers. However, successful business managers must realize that their customers often don't know what they want in the long term. Sometimes companies develop technologies before they are ready to be embraced by consumers. For example, cold-brew coffee took decades to become popular in the United States. The first commercial cold-brew coffee maker, the Toddy system, entered the market in 1964. [7] Yet it would take decades for cold-brew iced coffee to become popular. Today, it is found even in mass coffee chains like Starbucks. [8]

Key Takeaway 5

While market research is a key part of product development in large firms, it is impossible to do market research with customers and clients of new technologies.

Analysis

Customers cannot be surveyed about products that do not exist. New disruptive products create markets where there was no previous demand. For example, few customers in the early 1990s displayed much interest in digital music files, which emerged at a time when the sale of CD recordings remained profitable. Today, laptop computers often do not even come with a standard CD drive, because it's taken for granted that users will prefer digital music files instead.

The first commercial MP3 player entered the market in March 1998. [9] The MPMan F10 was manufactured by Saehan Information Systems, a South Korean firm. This was followed in September of that year by a similar player from California-based Diamond Multimedia, which introduced the Rio PMP300. Weary of the disruptive threat posed by portable music to CD and cassette sales, the Recording Industry Association of America sued Diamond Multimedia under the 1992 Audio Home Recording Act. [10] Less than a year later, in June 1999, Napster was founded. Napster was a peer-to-peer file sharing service that allowed users to share music online. The traditional music media industry did not immediately adapt to this disruptive change. As late as 2000, the sale of CD, vinyl, and cassette recordings represented well over 99 percent of global sales in music. [11] That same year, Napster reached 20 million users, and at its peak it would reach 57 million. Despite the fact that FIAA legal action effectively closed Napster that year, it had opened the way for a new industry and revolutionized music. [12] The MP3 was now a product people wanted. To take advantage of this new opportunity, Apple launched the iPod and its legal iTunes store in 2001. Digital music is now a ubiquitous feature of how people listen to music in the United States and a multibillion-dollar industry.

Key Takeaway 6

Market dynamics can favor new entrants into a business's sector at the expense of well-established firms.

Analysis

Entrenched firms tend to focus on their current market at the expense of developing customers in new sectors. Often, niche markets are too small for big firms to make a profit. In practice, this can mean that firms focused on new products can see very rapid rates of growth in markets that established firms cannot enter without diluting their brand.

Instead of refocusing on lower-end consumers or customers with niche needs, large luxury firms can contend with new innovations by purchasing promising rivals. An example of this strategy in practice is Facebook's purchase of WhatsApp in 2014. At the time of the purchase, Facebook had more users and its social network offered a number of ways for users to contact each other and share data.

WhatsApp offered only a fraction the modes of communication Facebook offered, but it was increasingly used by mobile phone users as a communications platform. In this way, WhatsApp's popularity posed a threat to Facebook's efforts to be the dominant communication platform. Recognizing the threat posed by WhatsApp, Facebook moved quickly to purchase it. [13]

Key Takeaway 7

Large companies are bureaucratic; innovation within them is often difficult as a result.

Analysis

Larger firms can fail to innovate for the simple reason that their size prohibits them from adapting quickly. Just as a trailer truck cannot turn as quickly as a modern sports car, large firms react more slowly to new innovations than smaller firms. Larger organizations are inherently more bureaucratic and it takes longer for ideas or values to be communicated across the entire organization. Managers of established large firms must be prepared in a way that does not compromise the company's values or its human resources. Employees may resent being tasked to work on an unproven and low-cost product. Employee performance may suffer if they are assigned to develop a less glamorous product.

Additionally, customers may not associate the company with the low-cost product or might expect the same level of service from the cheaper product. Firms can get around this by creating a new company if the original company's culture and brand value prevent it from taking advantage of these low-cost market opportunities. Firms can also re-brand some of their products to appeal to more cost-conscious consumers, or sell them under a slightly different name at a low-cost distributor. An example of this is the iconic breakfast cereal Cheerios, which is sold at the retailer Trader Joe's under the name "Joe's O's." [14]

Key Takeaway 8

Defectors who leave successful companies to start rival firms can be a serious challenge to the position of established firms in the market.

Analysis

When talented employees leave to start rival firms, they can develop innovations that threaten the hold established firms have over their customers. One example is Alan Shugart, who worked with IBM to launch the floppy drive industry before joining Memorex. Shugart went on to start two of his own companies: Shugart Associates and another firm that eventually became Seagate Technology. These companies brought new, cheaper products to market that threatened IBM and Memorex.

Another example is the so-called "traitorous eight" who left the technology firm Shockley Labs in the late 1950s to found Fairchild Semiconductor. This company was the progenitor of the Silicon Valley company Intel, and played an important role in the development of computer chips. [15] Outside the technology sector, David Neeleman and a number of former Southwest Airlines executives left that air carrier in 1998 to form a rival airline, JetBlue, which developed an innovative way to cut costs. [16] The success of these spin-off firms suggests that while large companies can incubate disruptive technologies, they often fail to bring them to market out of concern that emphasis on disruptive products will detract from more mainstream projects. Defectors with knowledge of these technologies can exploit them when they launch their own firms.

Author's Style

Clayton M. Christensen argues the book through case studies. Some, such as the discussion of the disk-drive industry, take up an entire chapter. Elsewhere, business case examples are as short as a few lines.

The book is an outgrowth of Christensen's doctoral thesis on the development of disk drives, which he published in 1993. As a result, the book has a dense academic tone in some sections. The author devotes long passages to the various aspects of different disk-drive technologies, which is very technically dense and difficult for the lay reader at times. These passages are made somewhat more accessible through the careful use of graphs. Photos in the text provide visual examples of some of the technologies the author mentions.

As this book is meant to appeal to a large number of business professionals, the author uses the term "technology" to apply to both technological innovation and business process innovation. Managers equipped with the theoretical business ideas in this book will be better prepared to adapt to disruptive changes.

Author's Perspective

Though his initial research was on the external disk-drive sector, Christensen believes his theory about disruptive innovation can be applied to almost any industry. When the book was first published in 1997, Christensen's argument went against traditional business management ideas that believed listening to customers and conducting research were the best ways to maintain the success of a firm.

A considerable portion of the book discusses the application of Christensen's theory to lower-technology industries such as mini-mill steel technology and mechanical excavators. The majority of products analyzed are those that are sold to other businesses. His case studies do not consider how issues such as regulation might have impacted the success of certain technologies or the long-term fate of companies.

~~~~ END OF INSTAREAD ~~~~

References

1. Suddath, Claire. "A Brief History of: Velcro." *Time,* June 15, 2010. Accessed April 4, 2016. content.time.com/time/nation/article/0,8599,1996883,00.html

2. Farrance, Rex. "Timeline: 50 Years of Hard Drives." *PC World,* September 13, 2006. Accessed April 4, 2016. www.pcworld.com/article/127105/article.html

3. Computer History Museum. "1980: Seagate 5.25-inch HDD becomes PC standard." Accessed April 16, 2016. www.computerhistory.org/storageengine/seagate-5-25-inch-hdd-becomes-pc-standard/

4. Farrance.

5. Ulanoff, Lance. "Say Goodbye to 3.5-inch Floppy Disks." *PC Magazine,* February 27, 2003. Accessed April 4, 2016. www.pcmag.com/article2/0,2817,905379,00.asp

6. Moscaritolo, Angela. "Sony Says Farewell to Betamax Cassettes." *PC Magazine,* November 10, 2015. Accessed March 16, 2016. www.pcmag.com/article2/0,2817,2494845,00.asp

7. "Toddy Cold Brew System." Toddy. Accessed March 13, 2016. https://toddycafe.com/toddy-cold-brew-system

8. Giammona, Craig. "Starbucks to Introduce Cold Brew Coffee at 2,800 U.S. Cafes." Bloomberg, March 12, 2015. Accessed April 4, 2016. www.bloomberg.com/news/articles/2015-03-12/starbucks-will-introduce-cold-brew-coffee-at-2-800-u-s-cafes

9. Smith, Tony. "Ten years old: the world's first MP3 player." *The Register*, March 10, 2008. Accessed April 12, 2016. www.theregister.co.uk/2008/03/10/ft_first_mp3_player/

10. Ibid.

11. International Federation of the Phonographic Industry. "2000 recording industry world sales." April 9, 2001. Accessed April 12, 2016. http://www.ifpi.org/content/library/worldsales2000.pdf

12. Lamont, Tom. "Napster: the day the music was set free." *The Guardian*, February 23, 2013. Accessed April 12, 2016. www.theguardian.com/music/2013/feb/24/napster-music-free-file-sharing

13. Hartung, Adam. "Three Smart Lessons From Facebook's Purchase Of WhatsApp." *Forbes*, February 24, 2014. Accessed March 16, 2016. www.forbes.com/sites/adamhartung/2014/02/24/zuckerbergs-3-smart-leadership-lessons-from-facebook-buying-whatsapp/#1e6251411d91

14. Aiken, Kristen. "Who Really Makes Trader Joe's Food?" *The Huffington Post*, January 23, 2014. Accessed April 4, 2016. www.huffington-post.com/2013/02/12/who-makes-trader-joes-food_n_2664899.html

15. Morris, Rhett. "The First Trillion-Dollar Startup." *TechCrunch*, July 26, 2014. Accessed April 4, 2016. techcrunch.com/2014/07/26/the-first-trillion-dollar-startup/

16. Brizek, Michael. "JetBlue Airways, Trouble in the Sky." *Journal of Aviation Management and Education*, 2010, 1, 1-13, p. 2. Accessed March 15, 2016. www.aabri.com/manuscripts/10478.pdf

CPSIA information can be obtained
at www.ICGtesting.com
Printed in the USA
BVOW08s1500171117
500588BV00010B/169/P